This SPECIAL STORIES BOOK Belongs To:

_____

Published in 2009 by
Special Stories Publishing

Member of CLÉ – The Irish Book Publishers Association

Design by Graham Thew Design www.grahamthew.com

ISBN 978 0 9561751 0 6

A catalogue record for this book is available from the British Library

Printed by C&C Offset Printing Co, Ltd, China

 Special Stories Publishing
www.specialstories.ie

TOM'S SPECIAL
TALENT

By Kate Gaynor

Illustrated by Eva Byrne

Hi! My name is Tom.

My school is a big yellow building right in the middle of Firswood, the town where I live. There are lots of other boys and girls in my class as well as my teacher, of course. Her name is Miss Jolly.

Miss Jolly is a great teacher. Every day we learn something different and exciting. Like today when we learned all about the world's famous artists and where they live.

There are some parts of Miss Jolly's class that I enjoy more than others. I love when Miss Jolly plays her guitar and we sing songs or paint pictures with our big thick paint brushes.

The only part of the school day I don't really like is when we practise our reading and writing. This is the part of the day that I think is kind of hard. Miss Jolly says that reading and writing are an important part of going to school and that is why we spend a lot of time practising these things in the class room.

When it's my turn to read from a book or from the board, I feel worried and afraid that I might get the words wrong. I am not as good at reading as some of my friends.

Miss Jolly says that all boys and girls have very different ways of learning. Some people find learning harder to do than others, but we all have special talents that are unique to us. "Just look around the classroom at all of your friends," said Miss Jolly, "Everyone has a special talent for something!"

When someone finds reading, writing or spelling hard
to do, this is sometimes called 'dyslexia'. It doesn't mean
that you are not as clever as your friends. It just means
that you have to practise a bit harder at the things
you find difficult to do.

I'm good at playing games.

Singing songs.

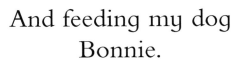

And feeding my dog Bonnie.

My Dad says it's easy to be good at things when you practise a lot.

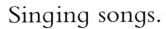

One day at school, our school principal Mrs. Berry made a surprise announcement. "Our big yellow school is going to be 50 years old next Wednesday!" she said. "So next week we will have a 'Celebrate our School' competition!"

"All the boys and girls will have to use their talents to create something they think celebrates their time at school." "Then, the very best story, poem or painting will be printed in the local newspaper where everyone will see it," explained Mrs. Berry.

When we all went back to class, everyone was talking
about the competition and who the winner might be.
Later that day I had my special reading time with Miss
Jolly. During this time we use lots of different ways
to help me learn my words and spellings.

But that day, instead of reading and spellings, we talked about the big competition. "I think I would like to paint a picture of all my friends," I told Miss Jolly. "Showing how each and every one of us has a special talent." "That's a great idea Tom," said Miss Jolly.

Every day after school I worked hard on my poster. First I drew a giant square with a space for everyone in my class. There was John, who is not very good at writing but is great at football. Sadie who finds maths hard to do, but is great at reading! Jayne writing one of her stories and Greg writing one of his funny poems!

Very soon there was only one space left on the poster for me and my special talent. "I don't think I have a talent at all," I told my Mum sadly. "I'm not very good at reading like Sadie or writing like Jayne." "How about your talent for painting and drawing?" laughed Mum looking at my poster. "I suppose you're right Mum," I smiled. "I do have a special talent too!"

The next day at school we all gathered in our school hall and waited for our principal Mrs. Berry to decide the winner of the 'Celebrate our School' competition.

"And the prize goes to Tom and his wonderful poster of talents!" announced Mrs. Berry. "Maybe Tom will become a famous artist some day and I will tell my new pupils all about him," said Miss Jolly with a proud smile. All of my friends clapped and cheered. Mrs. Berry said that my poster showed everyone how important it is to have respect for other people's talents and weaknesses because those are the things that make us special.

Now it's over to you; why don't you tell me all about your special talent?

YOUR SPECIAL STORY PAGE

NOTES FOR GROWN UP'S:

DYSLEXIA IS A specific learning difficulty which primarily affects acquisition of reading, spelling, writing and sometimes maths. Particular signs to watch for include: reversals of letters or words, difficulty remembering things in sequence (i.e. days of the week, times tables), poor short-term memory, confusion with left and right and difficulty recalling words. Dyslexia is not a disease or a defect, merely a difference in various learning processes.

HOW TO USE THIS BOOK:

CHILDREN WITH dyslexia or a learning difficulty often find school a daunting and sometimes terrifying daily task. In an environment where certain skills, like writing and reading, are praised and highlighted more than others, it is important for children to recognise that everyone has a 'special talent' of their own. It encourages other children to be mindful of the differences that exist between their friends and classmates and to be aware that all children, regardless of their talent, learn differently.

THE DYSLEXIA ASSOCIATION OF IRELAND: Dyslexia is quite common, about 8% of the population have dyslexia. It is genetic therefore one is usually born with it, and it is lifelong. However, with early identification and appropriate teaching, children with dyslexia can learn strategies to circumvent the difficulties. They are then able to achieve their potential, which in many cases is considerable. Parents and teachers need to be aware of dyslexia, and know that with early identification, specialist teaching and lots of support and encouragement, each child with dyslexia will be successful and reach their full potential.

For information on dyslexia in Ireland please contact the Dyslexia Association of Ireland at **www.dyslexia.ie** or (01) 6790276. For information outside Ireland, please contact your local Dyslexia Association.

Acknowledgements:

Many thanks to the Special Stories Publishing advisory Board, Michael Gill, Sandra O'Malley, Aine Lynch, David Shaw, Fintan Maher, Paul Toner and to Social Entrepreneurs Ireland, Sean, Lynda, Claire and Annalisa for all of their encouragement, advice and unwavering support. Many thanks also to Kieran O'Donoghue, Michael & George Gaynor and our extended family and friends, Liam Gaynor, Liz O'Donoghue, Trevor Patterson and Eva Byrne, Graham Thew, James Fitzsimons,

Special Stories Publishing is supported by Social Entrepreneurs Ireland
www.socialentrepreneurs.ie

Special thanks to Rosie Bisset, Mary Ball and The Dyslexia Association of Ireland without whose involvement this book would have not been possible.

Special thanks also to Dr. Imelda Coyne, Trinity College Dublin whose time and effort with this project was so greatly appreciated.

About the Author:

Kate Gaynor is the author of 11 published children's books. Her titles address the issues of children with special education needs or health and social problems. She works closely with healthcare professionals, psychologists, teachers and families on a daily basis to ensure the quality of her work. Kate is an English and Sociology graduate of University College Dublin and lives and works in Dublin, Ireland

About the Illustrator:

Eva Byrne is a well-known illustrator of books such as "Food to Match Your Mood" "Being You" and "So New York". As well as illustrating book covers, newspapers and magazine articles, she has worked on numerous advertising campaigns both in Europe and the United States.

Other Books from SPECIAL STORIES PUBLISHING
The SPECIAL STORIES SERIES 2:

THE SPECIAL STORIES SERIES 2 - These books are designed to introduce all children to the positive aspects of inclusive education with each book featuring a character with a certain special education need. The stories help children to learn the importance of accepting friends and classmates who are 'different' to them.

A BIRTHDAY FOR BEN

Children with hearing difficulties. It's Ben's 7th birthday, but he really doesn't want a birthday party! When his friends surprise him, he then learns just how easy it is for everyone to join in the fun.

TOM'S SPECIAL TALENT

Dyslexia/Learning difficulties. Tom isn't sure if he really has any talents at all when he sees how good his friends are at reading and writing. But a school competition helps him to find his own very 'special talent'.

FREDDIE'S SUPER SUMMER

Down Syndrome. It's Freddie's very first time at summer camp and he's certain he won't enjoy it or make friends. But it isn't long before a boy called Jerry helps him to see otherwise!

A FRIEND LIKE SIMON:

Autism/ASD. When a new boy joins Matthew's school, he's just not sure if he wants to have a friend like Simon. But a school trip to the funfair soon helps to change his mind!

(Books are sold separately and/or as part of a box set)

The SPECIAL STORIES SERIES 1:

A FAMILY FOR SAMMY
Foster Care

FIRST PLACE
Cleft Palate & Speech difficulties

THE LOST PUPPY
Limited mobility/ wheelchair users

THE FAMOUS HAT
Childhood Cancer

JOE'S SPECIAL STORY
Inter-country Adoption

THE WINNER
Asthma

THE BRAVEST GIRL IN SCHOOL
Diabetes

(Books are sold separately and/or as part of a box set)

www.specialstories.ie

www.specialstories.ie